# The Crossing of The Jordan

Don Farmer, Jr.

# *DEDICATION*

**Rev. Don Farmer, Sr.**
At His Mother's Home in Elkhorn, W.Va. 1950

*The Crossing of The Jordan* is lovingly dedicated to the memory of my father, Rev. Don Farmer, Sr., a faithful minister, who for more than fifty years preached the Word of God without fear or favor in the hollows and hills of the coalfields of southern West Virginia.

He was a good soldier who served his country well in the U.S. Navy during World War II. He was a good husband who loved and cared for his wife. He was a hard worker who labored in the coal mines to provide for his family. He was a good father who trained up his children in the way that they should go.

On Tuesday, March 15, 2005 with his family at his bedside, he made *The Crossing* to join the many loved ones who wait for us on the other side of *The Jordan*. For those who knew him, the Land of Promise will now be ever dearer and more desirable.

# Introduction

The Crossing of the Jordan was preached several times in the Fall and Winter of 1999, looking forward to the coming of The New Year 2000. The anticipation of the beginning of a New Millenium, Y2K, was marked by great excitement and many fears.

There were serious concerns about world wide high level computer crashes. There were terrible scenarios of interruptions of government, military, banking, transportation, trucking, business and school systems resulting in debilitating irregularities of every kind at home and around the world. Plane crashes, missile launches, unplanned military engagements, loss of all records, loss of all monetary accounts and assets, identity loss, food shortages, riots and pandemonium were all seen as real possibilities.

As people looked forward to the Coming of The Year 2000, there was talk of The End of the World. Bible prophecies were being reviewed, and many anxiously awaited the Coming of Christ. As the old-timers would say, they stood ready to Cross over Jordan.

In that context it is very interesting to read in Joshua 3 how that after forty years of wandering in the wilderness, when the children of Israel finally stood ready for T*he Crossing of The Jordan,* their crossing also involved the number 2000.

Joshua 3:4, "Yet there shall be a space between you and it, about two thousand cubits by measure..." The Ark was to cross Jordan first. The people would follow two thousand cubits later.

Is there a message here for God's people today? Is it that Christ has first crossed the Jordan, or passed into the Heavens, while His people are waiting to follow Him two thousand years later?

This was a very exciting prospect as the world looked forward to January 1, 2000.

It is still a very exciting prospect when we consider that Israel in the wilderness, preparing to cross to Canaan, is a very clear picture of The Church in this age preparing to cross to Heaven, not 2000 years from the date of Christ's birth, but 2000 years from the date of His resurrection and ascension.

Although Y2K has come and gone, the message remains valid. It should be read and preached everywhere, in preparation for the coming of our Lord, and our gathering together unto Him,

The 2000th anniversary of His death, burial, resurrection and ascension will soon be upon us. It is time for His return.

According to the word of God, just any day there will be a trumpet, and a shout, and the Church of The Lord Jesus Christ will be called out to make The Crossing of The Jordan. Have you made your preparation?

Don Farmer, Jr.

# The Crossing Of The Jordan

Open your Bibles with me to the Old Testament book of Joshua. In Chapter Three, begin reading with verse number one:

*1. And Joshua rose early in the morning; and they removed from Shittim, and came to Jordan, he and all the children of Israel, and lodged there before they passed over.*
*2. And it came to pass after three days, that the officers went through the hosts;*
*3. And they commanded the people, saying When ye see the ark of the covenant of the LORD your God, and the priests the Levites bearing it, then ye shall remove from your place, and go after it.*
*4. Yet there shall be a space between you and it, about two thousand cubits by measure: come not near unto it, that ye may know the way by which ye must go for ye have not passed this way heretofore.*
*5. Sanctify yourselves: for tomorrow the LORD shall do wonders among you.*

The Bible is not a dull book. It is a very rich and exciting book. So often the richness of its simplest passages seem to be overwhelming. The verses we have just read are a good example.

The Old Testament, especially, is rich in types and shadows, in pictures of future things. God, in this kind of secret way, revealed long before the time, just what He would do in that day when He would send the promised Messiah.

Here in Joshua, chapter 3, we have a literal account

of an actual historical event, the preparation of the children of Israel for The Crossing Of The Jordan. On the surface is one story; just beneath the surface is a much bigger story.

## "And Joshua"

Notice how the narrative begins. The story begins with a person, and the person is Joshua. The name, Joshua, has great significance in the Hebrew language and text, for it is the Old Testament Hebrew name which corresponds with the New Testament Greek name, Jesus.

In the New Testament epistle to the Hebrews, chapter 4, verse 8, we find the words: "For if Jesus had given them rest, then would He not afterward spoken of another day." The Jesus referred to in this verse is not the Jesus of the New Testament, but actually, the Joshua of the Old Testament.

Why did the KJV translators use the name Jesus here? Because the name Jesus in the Greek, and the name Joshua in the Hebrew are the same name.

The name Joshua means "deliverer" or "saviour." It should not be difficult, then, to see that the earthly Joshua in our text pictures for us the Heavenly Joshua, our *deliverer,* our *Saviour,* the Lord Jesus Christ. Here, and elsewhere in the Word of God, the Old Testament Joshua is a very good type or picture of The New Testament Jesus.

## "rose early in the morning"

On the surface, this statement might only seem to indicate that Joshua was an early riser, or that he may have been anxious for the day's events. This would not have been unusual, knowing that nearly all of the men in scripture who walked with God rose up early in the morning to seek Him.

However, given that the earthly Joshua in this passage is a picture of the Heavenly Joshua, the Lord Jesus Christ, these words are very full of meaning. *"And Joshua rose up early in the morning."*

This one phrase reveals, in essence, the reason why the Heavenly Joshua was to come. The reason that the Lord Jesus Christ, the Son of God, came down from Heaven was so that He, bearing the sins of all humanity, might go to the cross of Calvary: there suffer, bleed and die; be buried in the garden tomb; and then, *early* one Easter morning *rise up* victorious, triumphant, over death, hell and the grave.

Mark's gospel is careful to tell us: "And very e*arly in the morning* the first day of the week, they came unto the sepulchre at the rising of the sun." (Mk. 16:2) It was not only the time of the rising of the *"sun,"* but the time of the rising of the *"son,"* the Son of God.

Luke's gospel says: "Now upon the first day of the week, *very early in the morning,* they came unto the sepulchre, bringing the spices which they had prepared; and certain others with them. And they found the stone rolled away from the sepulchre. And they entered in, and found the stone rolled away from the sepulchre. And they entered in, and found not the body of the Lord Jesus." (Luke. 24:1-

3) The phrase, "And Joshua rose early in the morning," certainly foreshadows, in these verses, the resurrection of the Lord Jesus Christ.

In fact, look back for just a moment, at Joshua 1:1-2: "Now after the death of Moses the servant of the LORD it came to pass, that the LORD spake unto Joshua the son of Nun, Moses' minister saying, Moses my servant is dead; now therefore arise, go over this Jordan, thou, and all this people, unto the land which I do give to them, even to the children of Israel.."

Here, we may look at **Moses**, *the servant of the LORD* as a picture of the "Law," remembering that John 1:17 says, "For the law was given by Moses, but grace and truth came by Jesus Christ."

Now notice Joshua 1:2, "Moses my servant *is dead.*" We might ask, when did the "Law" die?

The Law died when Jesus died. Colossians 2:14 says, "Blotting out the handwriting of ordinances that was against us, which was contrary to us, and took it out of the way, nailing it to His cross;"

*"Moses my servant is dead; now, therefore arise."*

In other words, now that Christ has gone to the cross, *now* that He has removed the Law as a barrier between God and man, *now* that the Law is no longer man's means of approach to God. Now that the Law is dead, He, Jesus, the Heavenly Joshua can *arise*. And history records that from the Garden Tomb He did exactly that!

And *now*, ". . .Christ is the end of the law for righteousness to every one that believeth." (Romans 10:4)

## "he and all the children of Israel"

Of course, this had been the LORD's command in chapter 1:2, "thou and all this people," that is, The Children of Israel. The Children of Israel, that nation which God had raised up for Himself, was His chosen covenanted people.

The Word of God is always careful to make the distinction between Israel and The Church. This distinction is key to rightly dividing the Word of God. Israel is God's earthly people, with earthly covenants, earthly promises, and an earthly inheritance. The Church is God's Heavenly people, with Heavenly covenants, Heavenly promises, and a Heavenly inheritance.

However, the New Testament confirms that the children of Israel in their wilderness journey, *Israel in the wilderness*, is a type or picture of The Church. Listen to the language of Acts 7:38, "This is he that was in *the church in the wilderness* with the angel which spake to him in the Mount Sina, and with our fathers: who received the lively oracles to give unto us:"

Just as the earthly Joshua in this account pictures the Heavenly Joshua, the Lord Jesus Christ; the children of Israel on the wilderness side of the Jordan picture or foreshadow the New Testament church, The Church of the Lord Jesus Christ.

Now think about the words of the text. "And Joshua rose early in the morning . . . he and all the children of Israel." In a spiritual way this text anticipates the New Testament teaching that when Christ would rise up from the grave, His Church would rise up with Him.

2 Corinthians 5:14 says, ". . . because we thus judge that if one died for all, then were all dead." Ephesians 2:4-6, says, "But God, who is rich in mercy, for his great love wherewith he loved us, even when we were dead in sins, hath quickened us together with Christ, (by grace ye are saved); and hath *raised us up together* and made us sit *together* in Heavenly places in Christ Jesus."

In the New Testament Church, Christ is the believer's substitute in His death, burial and resurrection. Positionally, "all the children" are crucified, buried and risen with Christ.

Colossians 3:1 adds, "If ye then be risen with Christ, seek those things which are above, where Christ sitteth on the right hand of God." The good news for the world is that Christ is risen. The good news for the Church is that "all the children" are risen with Him.

## "and they removed from Shittim"

Joshua rose up early in the morning, "and they removed from Shittim." Shittim is also called "Abel-shittim" (Num. 33:49). It was the plain in the land of Moab where the Israelites were encamped after they had defeated the kings, Sihon and Og. It was from here that Joshua sent forth two spies to view the land and Jericho (Joshua 2:1).

"Shittim" means acacias. The acacia is the gum-arabic tree, also called the "shittah" tree (Isaiah 41:19). Its wood is called shittim wood (Exodus 25:10,23; 26:15,26). The acacia tree, much like the hawthorn, is a gnarled and thorny tree.

The gnarled and thorny wood of the acacia tree speaks of the curse of God upon the earth because of man's sin. Remember what God said when Adam had disobeyed Him in the garden.

"And unto Adam He said, Because thou hast hearkened unto the voice of thy wife, and hast eaten of the tree, of which I commanded thee saying, Thou shalt not eat of it: cursed is the ground for thy sake; in sorrow shalt thou eat of it all the days of thy life; thorns also and thistles shall it bring forth to thee; and thou shalt eat the herb of the field; in the sweat of thy face shalt thou eat bread, till thou return unto the ground; for out of it wast thou taken, for dust thou art, and unto dust shalt thou return." (Gen. 3:17-19)

"*Thorns and thistles* shall it bring forth to thee." From that day until this, the *"thorn"* is a reminder that because of man's sin, the earth is under the curse of God. Shittim, then, the place of the "acacias," the place of the "thorns," was a place which symbolizes in our text the place of the curse of God upon man's sin. But Joshua 3:1 says that when "Joshua rose early in the morning . . . *they removed from Shittim.*"

Thank God, when Jesus Christ, the Heavenly Joshua rose up out of death three days after Calvary, He brought His Church out of Shittim. He removed His Church from the place of the curse of sin.

Galatians 3:16 says, "Christ hath redeemed us from the curse of the law, being made a curse for us: for it is written, cursed is every one that hangeth on a tree:" In His death for us upon the cross, Jesus was made *a curse for us*. In His resurrection, He came out of the place of the curse, and brought every believer out from under the curse with Him.

## "and came to Jordan"

"And Joshua rose early in the morning; and they removed from Shittim, and came to Jordan."

Jordan, of course, refers to the area of the Jordan river several miles due west of Shittim, and just north of where the river makes its entrance into the Dead Sea.

The name Jordan means "descender," or "flowing swiftly down," a reference to the descent which the river makes beginning high on the slopes of Mount Hermon in the north and reaching to the plains in the south.

The Jordan river descends, plunging swiftly downward from its mountain heights, and winds turn after turn like a bright green ribbon through an otherwise barren wasteland.

Like the description of the river of life in the Book of Revelation, on either side of the banks of the Jordan there are trees and areas of plush vegetation.

The scripture records that even in Abraham's day, "And Lot lifted up his eyes, and beheld all the plain of Jordan, that it was well watered every where, before the LORD destroyed Sodom and Gomorrah, even as the garden of the LORD, like the land of Egypt, as thou comest unto Zoar." (Gen. 13:10)

The message of the Jordan river is simple: out of death, life. The Jordan river makes life possible where otherwise there would be no life.

This was the very place our Lord Jesus came to demonstrate His mission and purpose for coming into this world.

"Then cometh Jesus from Galilee to Jordan unto John, to be baptized of him. But John forbad Him, saying I have need to be baptized of thee, and comest thou to me? And Jesus answering said unto him, Suffer it to be so now: for thus it becometh us to fulfil all righteousness. Then he suffered him. And Jesus, when He was baptized went up straightway out of the water: and, lo the heavens were opened unto Him, and He saw the Spirit of God descending like a dove, and lighting upon Him: And lo a voice from heaven, saying, This is my beloved Son, in whom I am well pleased." (Matthew 1:13-17)

Jesus did not go into the waters of the Jordan river in order to become a son of God. He was already the Son of God before He went to the Jordan. He did not go down into the Jordan to wash away sins. Jesus Christ, the virgin-born Son of God, had no sins to wash away. This is not, and never was the purpose of baptism.

He went down into the Jordan river to demonstrate His purpose for coming into a barren desert wasteland of sin. He descended into the Jordan and came up again, showing that He had come to bring life out of death.

Baptism pictures death, burial and resurrection. Romans 6:3-4 says, "Know ye not that so many of us as were baptized into Jesus Christ were baptized into his death? Therefore we are buried with him by baptism into death: that like as Christ was raised up from the dead by the glory of the Father, even so we also should walk in *newness of life*." The Jordan, then, pictures that place of life out of death, that place of *newness of life*.

Put it all together now. "And Joshua rose early in

the morning; and they removed from Shittim, and came to Jordan, he and all the children of Israel . . ."

How full of New Testament meaning are these few Old Testament words. What a picture of Jesus, the Heavenly Joshua, who having gone to the cross and to the tomb, rose up early in the morning: He and all His Church with Him. He brought them out from the place of the curse of sin, and brought them into the place of *newness of life*.

## "and lodged there before they passed over"

Joshua and the children of Israel came to the Jordan, and lodged there before they passed over. As they had done so many times before, during their wilderness journey, they set up camp.

Always before they had waited for the cloud to move, and they followed the cloud. This time they were moving upon direct orders from Jehovah.

"Moses my servant is dead; now therefore arise, go over this Jordan, thou, and all this people, unto the land which I do give to them, even to the children of Israel." (Joshua 1:2)

So they came to Jordan, and "lodged" there before they passed over.

The word "lodged" used here is an interesting word. Most often in scripture it means only to spend the night.

Travelers, then as now, as evening shadows faded into darkness would seek a place where they could rest and be refreshed from the hardships of the journey. Here they would find shelter from the dangers which lurked in the darkness. They would spend only the night for their desire and full intention would be to turn homeward in the morning when the sun appears.

Certainly this speaks of the pilgrim character of the Church which lodges here in the darkness of this world of sin with all its dangers on every hand. For the Church, the night will grow ever darker and ever more dangerous with its coming apostasy, leading toward the rise and reign of the man of sin. Here she must spend the night, but she will spend only the night. Her full intention is to turn homeward in the morning, when the "son" appears.

Though the word "lodge" most often means only to spend the night, it can also mean to make a brief stay, to temporarily dwell or sojourn; and this proved to be the case for the Children of Israel. They did camp by the Jordan more than one night.

The Hebrew word for "lodged" used in this text is a strange word in some ways. It literally means to lodge or stay *with obstinance*. There is in the word the sense of being obstinate or stubborn, of complaining, of having to endure the stay. It gives the idea of having to stay against one's will. They were stopping here, but they did not want to stop here. Their true desire was to cross over the Jordan and into the land of promise.

In spite of the desire to enter Canaan, Israel at the Jordan "lodged there before they passed over."

When the application of this phrase is made to the Church, we see that the Church who with Christ has passed from death to life (John 5:24) must now for the present time "lodge" here in this world, or as we often say, on this side of Jordan.

The Church lodges here on this side of Jordan, but she does so, as it were, against her will. She does lodge here, but she does not really want to lodge here. Like Israel in the text, her promises, her possessions, her inheritance, her home is on the other side. Her true desire is to "pass over."

The old song writer had it right: "On Jordan's stormy bank I stand, and cast a wishful eye toward Canaan's fair and happy land where my possessions lie." The word "lodge" means to stay against one's will, and the implication is that they stayed only because they had to. Their stay was not out of desire, but out of necessity. How true this is for the Church.

The Apostle Paul wrote in Philippians 1:21-23, "For me to live is Christ, and to die is gain. But if I live in the flesh, this is the fruit of my labour: yet what I shall choose I wot not. For I am in a strait betwixt two, having a desire to depart and to be with Christ; which is far better: Nevertheless to abide in the flesh is more needful for you. And having this confidence I know that I shall abide and continue with you all for your furtherance and joy of faith;" Here is the heart's desire of the Apostle Paul, *"For I . . . desire to depart and to be with Christ. . . . Nevertheless to abide . . . is more needful for you."* His desire was to depart and be with Christ, but he was willing to lodge here as long as it was needful.

If the Church had her heart's desire, she would depart and be with Christ. However, for the present time it is more needful for her to *abide* or to *lodge* here on this side of Jordan. And for the present time there is a very important reason why her stay here is needful.

## "the officers went through the host, and they commanded the people saying... that ye may know the way by which ye must go"

Israel had to "lodge" on the wilderness side of the Jordan because there was a "host" of people who had to be "commanded" or instructed that there was a crossing to be made, and that they must make preparation for the crossing. They needed to know *"the way* by which ye must go."

The scripture records a census of over six hundred thousand men, not counting women and children, who survived the forty years in the wilderness.

Assuming each man had a wife, and each couple had at least two children, there would have been nearly two and one half million people there by very conservative estimates. There may have been many, many more.

There really was *a host*, a multitude of people who needed to hear the message that the Jordan was to be crossed, and they needed to know ***the way*** to make the crossing.

In order to make the crossing, preparations had to be made, certain requirements had to be met, and they had to receive instruction concerning ***"the way."***

Notice whose responsibility it was to see that this was carried out, "the officers."

The dictionary defines "officer" as one who holds an office of authority, or one who holds a commission in the armed forces. Officers are men who have been commissioned by the Commander-in-Chief, and who serve under his authority.

How this does speak of the work of the New

Testament Church. In the Church, believers are God's *"officers"* invested with the authority of the Commander-in-Chief Himself, to carry out the Great Commission.

That commission in His own words is: "Go ye therefore, and teach all nations, baptizing them in the name of the Father, and of the Son, and of the Holy Ghost: Teaching them to observe all things whatsoever I have commanded you: and, lo I am with you alway, even unto the end of the world. Amen." (Matthew 28:19-20) Mark 16:15 records it this way: "And He said unto them, Go ye into all the world, and preach the gospel to every creature."

The *"officers"* going through *"the host"* making known *"the way"* to cross over Jordan picture for us the Church going "into all the world" with the gospel of Jesus Christ making known "the way" for men to get ready to make the crossing from this world to Heaven.

## "When ye see the ark . . . then ye shall . . . go after it."

Not only did the officers have a mission, they had a message, a message for the children of Israel, as they waited, desiring to enter in upon their inheritance, longing to know *the way*.

The message was simple: "When ye see the ark of the covenant of the LORD your God, and the priests the Levites bearing it, then ye shall remove from your place and go after it." (Josh. 3:3) When ye see The Ark, go after it.

"When ye see the Ark." For Israel to see the Ark would mean to perceive it visually. For the Church it would mean to perceive it with the mind or with the heart. To "see" the Ark would mean not only to behold the Ark with the eyes, but to understand what the Ark represented. It would mean to see and to understand *The Message of the Ark*.

The *Message of the Ark* was two-fold. One message was obvious in **The Purpose and Use of the Ark** in the priestly service at the Tabernacle. A second less obvious message was to be found in **The Symbolism of the Ark**.

**The Purpose and Use of the Ark** at the tabernacle reveals The Message of The Blood Atonement. The Ark of the Covenant of the Lord God of Israel with its Mercy Seat, its Sacrificial Blood of Sprinkling, and the Intercessory Ministry of its Great High priest reveals for all time sinful man's *only way* of approach to a Holy God.

Exodus 25 gives the *blueprint* for the construction of the Ark and the Mercy Seat: 10. "And they shall make an Ark of shittim wood: two cubits and a half shall be the length thereof, and a cubit and a half the breadth thereof, and a cubit and a half the height thereof. 17. And thou shalt make a Mercy Seat of pure gold: two cubits and a half shall be the length thereof, and a cubit and a half the breadth thereof.. 21. And thou shalt put the Mercy Seat above upon the Ark; and in the Ark thou shalt put the testimony that I shall give thee. 22. And there I will meet with thee, and I will commune with thee from above the Mercy Seat, from between the two cherubims which are upon the Ark of the testimony, of all things which I will give thee in commandment unto the children of Israel. . ."

*The Purpose of the Ark* and the Mercy Seat is explained in Leviticus 16:9. "And Aaron shall bring the goat upon which the Lord's lot fell, and offer him for a sin offering. 15. Then shall he kill the goat of the sin-offering, that is for the people, and bring his blood within the vail . . . and sprinkle it upon the mercy seat, and before the mercy seat: 16. And he shall make an atonement for the holy place, because of the uncleanness of the children of Israel, and because of their transgressions in all their sins; and so shall he do for the tabernacle of the congregation, that remaineth among them in the midst of their uncleanness. 34. And this shall be an everlasting statute unto you, to make an atonement for the children of Israel for all their sins once a year. . ."

*The Message of the Ark* is clear. There can be no approach to God, no fellowship with God, no right standing before God, and no preparation to meet God without the Blood of a Sin Offering, offered sacrificially, and sprinkled by the High priest upon the Mercy Seat of the Ark of God in the Holy of Holies.

For Israel in the Old Testament the message was one sacrifice for all Israel for one year. (Leviticus 16:34) Hebrews 10 quotes Psalm 40, and speaks of a day when there would be "one sacrifice for sins for ever" for all men. (Hebrews 10:5-12)

*The Message of The Ark* is made even clearer when we consider **The Symbolism of The Ark**. *The Symbolism of The Ark* does not reveal a different message, but the same message told in a different way. *The Symbolism of The Ark* in every way reveals the person and work of Jesus Christ, The Minister of "The True Tabernacle which The Lord pitched, and not man." (Hebrews 8:2)

The Ark pictures Christ Pre-existent. The Ark was commissioned and built first of all the furnishings of the Tabernacle. Chronologically, at the Tabernacle, the Ark predated everything else. Colossians 1:17 says about Jesus, "And He is before all things, and by Him all things consist."

The Ark pictures Christ Prophesied. The ark was foreseen and foretold in Exodus 25:8-10, although it did not become a physical reality until its construction sometime later in Exodus 37:1-5. In the same way, Christ was foreseen and foretold by the prophets in the Old Testament, many, many years before His actual appearance in the gospels at the beginning of the New Testament.

The Ark pictures Christ as the Incarnate Word of God. The tables of law inside the Ark, inscribed by God Himself before the Ark was ever made, reveal Christ as the Word who was in the beginning with God, and who was God. (John 1:1)

The Ark pictures Christ as Immanuel. The Ark was fashioned as the place where God dwelled with Man. (Exodus 25:22) In the same way we see Christ as the person in which God dwelled with man. Immanuel means "God with us." (Isaiah 7:14) "And the Word was made flesh and dwelt among us, and we beheld His glory, the glory as of the only begotten of the Father, full of grace and truth. (John 1:14)

The Ark pictures Christ born of a virgin. The Ark, like the tabernacle, was made of very wide boards. The wooden furnishing of the tabernacle were made of acacia or shittim wood which come from a naturally small tree. Dimension for the boards of the tabernacle were "a cubit and a half" in width by "ten cubits" in length. (Ex. 26:16) Boards of this size could only come from very large acacia trees, trees which had never before been cut, trees never before touched by human hands or man-made instruments. Such trees are always referred to as "virgin timber." This, certainly, speaks of Christ's virgin birth. Isaiah 7:14 reads, ". . . Behold a virgin shall conceive, and bear a son, and shall call His name Immanuel."

The Ark pictures Christ conceived by the Holy Spirit. The Ark was fashioned by a man named Bezaleel. Exodus 37:1 says, "And Bezaleel made the ark of shittim wood:" The Hebrew name Bezaleel means "in the shadow of God." The Ark was fashioned by Bezaleel, or literally, by or in "the shadow of God." It is by no coincidence that we read in Luke Chapter 1, the words of the angel Gabriel to the virgin Mary, ". . . The Holy Ghost shall come upon thee, and the power of the Highest shall *overshadow* thee: therefore also that holy thing which shall be born of thee shall be called the son of God." The virgin Mary was *overshadowed* by the Holy Ghost, and Jesus, in His humanity, was literally formed like the ark, in *the shadow of God.*

The Ark pictures Christ's humanity and deity. The wood of the Ark, acacia wood, the gnarled and twisted wood of the desert, pictures Christ as "the root out of dry ground" (Isaiah 53:2), the "rod out of the stem of Jesse," the "Branch . . . out of his roots," and speaks of His humanity. Everywhere in scripture gold is symbolic of royalty and deity. It is the metal of the furnishings of the tabernacle. The pure gold of the Ark speaks of Christ's deity. Without ceasing to be God, He became man. (Philippians 2:6-8) He is God manifest in human flesh. He is the God Man.

The Ark pictures Christ's sinlessness. The Ark was the holiest piece of furniture in the tabernacle. The Ark stood alone in the Holy of Holies. So Christ stands alone as the one-and-only-one truly Holy in a world of sinful men. Hebrews 4:15 says that He "was in all points tempted like as we are, yet without sin." Hebrews 7:26 says, "For such an high priest became us, who is holy, harmless, undefiled, separate from sinners, and made higher than the heavens."

The Ark pictures Christ's passion. The covering of the Ark with its cherubims and mercy seat speaks to us emphatically of Christ's sufferings. Exodus 25:18 says, "And thou shalt make two cherubims of gold, of *beaten* work shalt thou make them, in the two ends of the mercy seat." Exodus 37:7 adds, "And he made two cherubims of gold, *beaten* out of one piece made he them, on the two ends of the mercy seat." The gospels, of course, tell how our Lord was severely beaten before He ever went to Calvary. "And so Pilate, willing to content the people, released Barabbas unto them and delivered Jesus, *when he had scourged Him*, to be crucified." (Mark 15:15) And as Matthew 27:36 was careful to record: "they spit upon Him, and took the reed, *and smote Him* on the head." "But he was wounded for our transgressions, he was bruised for our iniquities: the chastisement of our peace was upon him; and with his stripes we are healed." (Isaiah 53:5)

The Ark pictures Christ's crucifixion. The rings and staves of the Ark speak of His crucifixion. A ring was made into each corner of the ark. Along each side a rod or stave was slid through the rings, so that it could be transported or carried by the priests. The staves passed through the two rings on each side just as the nails passed through His two hands and two feet. Just like the Ark was always "lifted up" when it was carried, the Lord Jesus was "lifted up" (John 12:32) on the cross to bear our griefs and to carry our sorrows. (Isaiah 53:4)

The Ark pictures Christ's burial, because the same Hebrew word used everywhere in the word of God for the Ark of the Covenant is in Genesis 50:26 translated "coffin." In this verse, Joseph, one of the most clear and perfect types of Christ in the Old Testament, has died, and is put in an '"ark" or "coffin" in Egypt, looking forward to the day when he will be carried up out of Egypt to the land of promise. Paul says in I Corinthians 15: 3-4, "For I delivered unto you first of all that which I also received, how that Christ died for our sins according to the scriptures; *And that He was buried. . .*" Isaiah 53:9 prophesies, "And He made his grave with the wicked, and with the rich in His death. . ." The Lord Jesus in His death was buried in a grave in anticipation of the day He would rise up out of Death and pass into the Heavens.

The Ark pictures Christ's resurrection from the dead. The rod of Aaron inside the Ark speaks clearly of death and resurrection. The rod of Aaron, nothing more than a stick of wood, when laid, dead and dried before the presence of the Lord, "budded and brought forth buds, and bloomed blossoms, and yielded almonds." (Numbers 17:8) In the same way, Jesus, the rod of Jesse (Isaiah 11:1) was laid dead and cold, in the garden tomb, but on the third day He came to life again.

The Ark pictures Christ's ascension as High Priest to intercede for saints. On the Day of Atonement it was before the Holy Ark that the High Priest placed the golden censer filled with sweet incense. It spoke of the sweetness of Christ's sacrifice of Himself unto God. The cloud of incense before the Ark rose up from the censer and ascended as a sweet fragrance into the presence of Him who dwelled between the Cherubims. (Exodus 29:41) Likewise Christ ascended into the Heavens to intercede for men before the face of Jehovah.

The Ark pictures Christ's blood shed for the remission of sin. (Hebrews 9:22) The covering of gold with the Cherubims of Glory was referred to as the Mercy seat. This Mercy seat was the place of sprinkling of the blood of the sacrifice offered on the Day of Atonement. The blood on the Mercy seat was "to make an atonement for the children of Israel for all their sins once a year." (Leviticus 16:34) The blood on the Mercy seat of the Ark, speaks of Christ's "one sacrifice for sins forever." (Hebrews 10:12) "Neither by the blood of goats and calves, but by His own blood he entered in once into the holy place, having obtained eternal redemption for us." (Hebrews 9:12)

The Ark pictures Christ's Lordship, and looks forward to His future appearing. The crown of gold atop the Ark (Exodus 25:11) is not a victor's crown, but a diadem.

It is the crown of Christ's nobility, His royalty and His Lordship. On the cross Pilate's superscription read, Jesus of Nazareth King of the Jews. The scriptures are clear. He is

King. Paul wrote to Timothy, ". . . until the appearing of our Lord Jesus Christ: which in His times He shall shew, who is the blessed and only Potentate, the King of kings, and Lord of lords; (I Timothy 6:15)

The Ark pictures Christ, the Bread of Life. The golden pot of manna which Moses commanded to be placed inside the Ark reveals the Lord Jesus as the "Bread which cometh down from Heaven, that a man may eat thereof, and not die. (John 6:50)

*The Message of the Ark* was then, and is now, in every way the Message of Christ. Christ, the Pre-Existent One; Christ, the Prophesied one; Christ, the Incarnate Word; Christ, the Virgin Born Son; Christ, the Sinless One; Christ, the Suffering One; Christ, Crucified; Christ Buried, Christ, Resurrected; Christ, the Atoning Sacrifice. Christ, the Interceding High Priest; Christ, the King of Kings. Christ, the Lord of Lords; Christ, the Bread of Heaven which gives eternal life.

*"When ye see the Ark...go after it."* This was The Message of the officers to the host. This was in actuality *"the way by which ye must go."* (vs.4) In other words, the people were to understand that they must put their faith and trust in the Ark, that is in the shed blood on the Mercy Seat of the Ark. That Blood, and That Blood alone, sprinkled by their High priest upon that Mercy seat in the Holy place, could get them out of the barren desert wasteland, across the Jordan, and safe home to Canaan.

*"When ye see the Ark . . . go after it."* For Israel the message was when you see the Ark, with the Atoning Blood, and understand what it represents, then, go after it, follow it,

for it is *the way by which ye must go.*

In the same way today, we understand that Christ is *"the way by which ye must go."* Men must put their faith and trust in Him, and Him alone, in His Blood, and His Blood alone. Only the Blood of Jesus, sprinkled by Christ Himself on the Mercy seat in the Holy Place before the throne of God can get men out of the wilderness of sin, and across the swelling tide, and safe home to Heaven.

*"When ye see the ark . . . go after it."* For the church, the message simply put is, When you hear and understand the message that only The Blood of Jesus Christ can save men from sin: *go after it,* follow it, accept it, believe it, appropriate it, by putting your full faith and trust in Him and in His Blood.

## "When ye see the ark . . . then ye shall remove from your place, and go after it."

This phrase makes known to us the three requirements for salvation. It also reveals to us the three reasons why most men do not get saved.

Requirement No. 1 — *"When ye see the ark."* Israel had to see the Ark in order to make the crossing. So men must hear and understand The Message of the Ark, that is, The Message of the Blood Atonement, in order to be saved. They must put their full faith and trust in the sufficiency of The Blood of Christ to save them.

Ephesians 2:8-9 says, "For by grace are ye saved through faith; and that not of yourselves: it is the gift of

God: not of works, lest any man should boast." Romans 10:17 adds, "So then faith cometh by hearing, and hearing by the word of God." In order for men to be saved, they must hear the gospel message. This explains why so many are not saved. Many never hear the message.

Romans 10:8 says, "The word is nigh thee, even in thy mouth, and in thy heart: that is the word of faith which we preach; that if thou shalt confess with thy mouth the Lord Jesus, and shalt believe in thy heart that God hath raised him from the dead, thou shalt be saved. For with the heart man believeth unto righteousness; and with the mouth confession is made unto salvation. For the scripture saith, Whosoever believeth on him shall not be ashamed. For there is no difference between the Jew and the Greek: for the same Lord over all is rich unto all that call upon him. For whosoever shall call upon the name of the Lord shall be saved."

What a wonderful promise! Salvation is for all who will hear the word, believe the word and call upon the name of the Lord. However, listen to the questions in verses 14 and 15: "How then shall they call on Him in whom they have not believed? And how shall they believe in Him of whom they have not heard? And how shall they hear without a preacher? And how shall they preach, except they be sent?" Some are never saved because they never hear the gospel.

Some never hear the gospel because they never have a preacher, teacher, missionary or another Christian to tell them how to trust Christ in order to be saved.

Some never hear because they never listen. Some sit in Church week after week and hear the gospel preached, time after time, but pay no attention to it. They hear with their ears, but not with their hearts.

Some never hear because they have preconceived notions about how to be saved. They listen to the message that all men are sinners and can only be saved by the Blood of Jesus and the Grace of God; then tell themselves that because they are as good as other men, they too will surely be saved. They miss it altogether.

Some never hear because they have put their trust in their religious or secular affiliations. They think that they do not need a personal faith in Christ or the gospel.

But men must hear and believe the gospel in order to be saved. They must "see the Ark." They must understand that salvation is in the shed Blood of Christ. They must trust Him alone, and receive Him for salvation.

<u>Requirement No. 2</u> — *"then ye shall remove from your place."* If men want to be saved, when they hear a clear presentation of the gospel, they must "remove" from their place. Men must be willing to leave where they are and come to Christ. This means, of course, that men must be willing to leave that state of life, that place of condemnation in which they find themselves without Christ. They must be willing to turn away from the old life. They must be willing to leave the world behind them. They must be willing to die out to sin.

The scripture tells us "And this is the condemnation, that light is come into the world, and men loved darkness rather than light, because their deeds were evil. For every one that doeth evil hateth the light, neither cometh to the light, lest his deeds should be reproved. (John 3:19-20)

Some never get saved because they love darkness

rather than light. They have no interest in God or godly living. Some are not willing to leave where they are, and come to Christ. They are never saved because they love their sin and are not willing to turn from it. Some are never saved because they are wrapped up in the things of this life. They are satisfied with what they are, and where they are, and desire no other lifestyle.

The scripture is clear, however, "Except ye repent (remove from your place), ye shall all likewise perish." (Luke 13:1-5) The message of John the Baptist was the message of Christ Himself: "repentance for the remission of sins." (Luke 3:3) Peter repeats it, "Repent. . . for the remission of sins," (Acts 2:38) and again "Repent ye therefore, and be converted, that your sins may be blotted out." (Acts 3:19)

Proverbs 28:13, "He that covereth his sins shall not prosper: but whoso confesseth and forsaketh them shall have mercy." Romans 6:6, "Knowing this, that our old man is crucified with him, that the body of sin might be destroyed, that henceforth we should not serve sin."

If men are to be saved they must be willing to to confess and to forsake sin. They must be willing to die out to self. Men must be willing to "remove from" their own place, and go with God.

<u>Requirement No. 3</u> — *"and go after it."* If men are to be saved, they must not only hear the gospel, and turn from sin, but they must be willing from that day forward to "go after" Christ.

In the primary class we used to sing: "I have decided to follow Jesus. I have decided to follow Jesus. I have decided to follow Jesus. No turning back. No turning back."

In John 1:35-37 the Bible says, "Again the next day after John stood, and two of his disciples; And looking upon Jesus as he walked, he saith, Behold the Lamb of God! And the two disciples heard Him speak, and they *followed Him*."

That man who would be saved must begin a new life of following Jesus. This means that he will obey him, that he will do his will. This means that from that moment on Jesus in his heart becomes the Lord of his life.

Some people are never saved because they are not willing to follow Christ. There are some who have heard the gospel and have even believed that it is true. There are some who would even like to remove from where they are, because sin has gotten them into so much trouble, but they are not ready to commit to a life under the Lordship of Jesus Christ.

Some are never saved because they only want Jesus as a fire escape from hell. They do not want Him as the new Master over the daily activities of their lives. They want Him as Saviour, but they do not want Him as Lord.

He will not be Saviour without being Lord. When Jesus is referred to as Lord and Saviour, in the New Testament, "Lord" always appears first in the title, because He is, first of all, Lord.

"When ye see the ark . . . remove from your place, and go after it."

The requirements for salvation are that men hear the gospel and understand it, that they be willing to trust the shed blood of Christ alone as the atonement for their sin, that they be willing to turn completely from sin, and to receive, and to faithfully follow Christ.

For Israel there was nothing on the desert side of that river that was more attractive to them, or which presented a brighter prospect to them, than forsaking all else and following the Ark as it led them safely to their inheritance on the other side of the Jordan.

May God Almighty help men in this evil day to see that there is nothing in this sinful world which is more attractive, or which presents a brighter prospect than forsaking all else and following Christ to that "inheritance which is incorruptible and undefiled, and that fadeth not away, reserved in Heaven for you." (I Peter 1:4)

## "that ye may know"

Notice the New Testament language found in this Old Testament phrase: *"that ye may know."*

The people were being commanded, instructed in order that they might *know* God's way of salvation. God never leaves men in the dark concerning the matter of salvation. The word "ignorant" is found twelve times in the New Testament Epistles. In every case it is a condition to be disdained. The word "know" is found in the New Testament two hundred and seventy six times. God wants men ***to know*** the truth. Jesus said, "And ye shall **know** the truth, and the truth shall make you free." (John 8:32)

"That ye may know *the way*." This is a good New Testament phrase: "the way." Christ Himself is *"the way."* In John 14:6 Jesus said to Thomas, "I am THE WAY, THE TRUTH and THE LIFE." Jesus is not a good way to Heaven.

Jesus is not a better way to Heaven. Jesus is not even the best way to Heaven. Jesus is the ONLY way to Heaven. He is "the way by which ye *must* go."

Anyone who would leave the wilderness and cross the Jordan to Canaan MUST go by the one and only way. Anyone who would leave this world of sin and cross the great divide to enter Heaven MUST go by the one and only way. That way is Christ Himself. Acts 4:12 says, "Neither is there salvation in any other: for there is none other name under heaven given among men, whereby we MUST be saved."

## "When ye see the ark. . . the priests, the Levites bearing it"

The priests, the Levites were by divine appointment the bearers of the Ark. The people were instructed to watch for its appearance. The word was: "Behold the Ark of the covenant of the Lord of all the earth passeth over before you into Jordan. (vs.11)

And so at the proper moment, in the fulness of time, the priests took up the Ark. With the High priest leading the procession, the Ark made its appearance, presented the Blood, made God available to the people, and then departed. The Ark passed over before the people "*into* the Jordan."

What a picture of the Lord Jesus! In the *fulness* of time (Galatians 4:4) He made His appearance, presented His Blood, made God available to the people and then departed. He passed over before the people *into* Heaven.

The command was: "When ye see the Ark." But it is

interesting to note that the people never did actually see the Ark. They sort of saw the Ark without really seeing the Ark. How was that possible?

Numbers 4:5-6 reveals that when the Ark was to be moved, Aaron and his sons were to spread over the Ark "a cloth wholly of blue." The Ark was covered, or vailed so that the Ark itself could not be seen. What the people did see was the shape of the Ark. The shape they saw was enough to convince them that the Ark was really beneath the vail.

In this way they received the Ark with its blood atonement wholly by faith and not by sight.

One reason His own people, and many others, did not accept or receive the Lord Jesus when He came into this world was because they could not see Him for who He really was. They saw Him vailed in flesh. They saw Him as no different than any other man. They could not see Him as the Lord from Heaven. (I Corinthians 15:47)

One day He took Peter, James and John "up into a high mountain apart," (Matthew 17:1-2) and there He pulled back the vail. "And was transfigured before them: and His face did shine as the sun, and His raiment was white as the light." They saw Him for who He really was. The people of Israel did not see Him in His glory. They had to accept Him by faith. They did not see *"the Ark,"* so to speak, but those who believed in Him saw enough to convince them that He really was who He said He was.

It is also interesting to note that only those on or near the front line of the host, actually saw the Ark when it made its appearance. Each other line of people was increasingly farther away from the Ark. "When ye see the ark" took on a new meaning for those who were farther from the front line. There was no way they could see the ark or even its vail with their own eyes.

How did those further back know that the Ark had ever made its appearance? Very simple.

The people on the first row told the people on the second row. The people on the second row told the people on the third row. The people on the third row told the people on the fourth row, and so on, all the way back to the people on the last row. Everyone in the host had to take someone's word for it, who took someone's word for it, who took someone's word for it, and so on, that the Ark had actually made its appearance.

This has been, and is now, the ongoing work of the Church in every generation. In this very same way each generation has passed on the message to each succeeding generation that Jesus Christ came, and made a way for all men to prepare for the crossing.

Notice that the people on the front row were so convinced and overjoyed about what they saw that when they told the people on the second row, the people on the second row were convinced that the Ark had really appeared.

The people on the second row were so convinced and overjoyed about what they had heard that when they told the people on the third row, the people on the third row were convinced that the Ark had really appeared.

The people on the third row were so convinced and overjoyed about what they had heard that when they told the people on the fourth row, the people on the fourth row were convinced that the Ark had really appeared, and so on to the last row.

May we today be so convinced and overjoyed about knowing Christ that our children and grandchildren will see in our own lives the evidence of true faith, and be so convinced that Jesus Christ and His wonderful salvation are real, that they too will be willing to remove from where they are, and go after Him.

## ". . . go after it. Yet there shall be a space between you and it . . ."

The command for the people was: When ye see the Ark, "ye shall remove from your place, and GO AFTER IT!" And this, we may be sure, the people were very anxious to do. They were, undoubtedly, so elated that NOW, after centuries of bondage in Egypt, and after forty years of wandering in the desert., that NOW, finally, the time had come to cross over the Jordan and to enter the Promised Land.

In the language of verse four, it is almost as if the LORD knows that when the time comes for the Ark to appear, the people will be standing, waiting, watching for the slightest glimpse of it. It is almost as if Jehovah anticipates the eager rush of the people to the Jordan at the first moment in which the Ark is sighted.

His command is: "GO AFTER IT!" But then He warns, "YET THERE SHALL BE A SPACE BETWEEN YOU AND IT!"

They were to watch for the Ark. They were to follow the Ark. They were to go after the Ark, BUT they could not follow close behind it. They had to follow the Ark at a distance. They had to put *a space* between them and the Ark.

The High Priest was going to take the Ark with the Blood, go down to the river, and pass over before the people *into* Jordan. (Joshua 3:11) The waters would roll back to open the way for the people to cross over. The people, however, could not cross *into* Jordan when the High Priest did. At the moment the High Priest made his crossing, Israel was still two thousand cubits from the Jordan. Their crossing would come sometime *after* His.

This is very reminiscent of the language of John 13:33 where Jesus said, "Little children, yet a little while I am with you. Ye shall seek me: and as I said unto the Jews, Whither I go, ye cannot come; so now I say to you." Simon Peter asked Him in verse 36, "Lord, whither goest thou?" Jesus answered him, "Whither I go, thou canst not follow me *now*: but thou shalt follow me *afterwards*."

In other words, Jesus was about to be offered up as a sacrifice for sin. As our great High Priest He was going to take His own blood, cross into Heaven, and open the way for His Church to follow Him to the other side. But like Israel and the High Priest at the Jordan, the Church could not go with Him when He crossed. They would have to follow Him at a distance. "Thou canst not follow me *now*, but thou shalt follow me *afterwards*."

The question is, when would the children of Israel be allowed to follow the High Priest and the Ark *into* the Jordan? The text says, "Yet there shall be a SPACE between you and it, about two thousand cubits by measure."

An examination of the word "space" proves to be very interesting. It is the Hebrew word, "rachoq" {raw-khoke'} from the Strong's word no. 7368. "Rachoq" is used, literally or figuratively, of place or time. It is used to mean: afar, abroad, afar off, long ago, of old, a space, a great while to come. It is very interesting to note that in Biblical usage the word "rachoq" may be used in reference to distance, but it primarily denotes "time."

It is also interesting to note that the word "cubit" is the Hebrew word 'ammah {am-maw'} from the Strong's word no. 517; which really means mamma or "mother." It makes sense when we realize that the word refers to the "mother unit" or "standard unit" of measure.

The space between the High Priest's crossing and the people's crossing involved two things: a distance of two thousand cubits, and the time required to travel that distance. Both ideas are inherent in the word "space."

For Israel at the Jordan, certainly, the word "space" marks out a *distance* between the High Priest's crossing and the crossing of the people. The space was to be two thousand standard units of distance, or two thousand cubits.

For the believer in the present age, the word "space" seems to mark out a *time* between the crossing of Christ, the Great High Priest, and the crossing of His Church. The time seems to be two thousand standard units of time, or two thousand years.

Ordinarily, any mention of assigning a time to the Church Age, or any date to Christ's coming for the Church draws sharp criticism. Yet in Joshua 3:4 a distance was assigned between the crossing of the Ark and the crossing of the people. And Joshua 3:4 does indicate that the High Priest would cross into Jordan, and that the people would cross two thousand cubits later.

This is not the only place in the scripture where the number *two thousand* is used in a prophetic way in relation to Christ's coming.

Of course, II Peter 3:8 says, "But, beloved, be not ignorant of this one thing, that one day is with the Lord as a thousand years, and a thousand years as one day." Notice how God measures time. One thousand years equals one day. On that same time scale, two thousand years equal two days. With this in mind, look in Luke 10:30-35 at the account of the good Samaritan.

When the priest and the Levite passed by the man who fell among thieves, they left him half dead and unaided. When the Good Samaritan passed by, he "went to him and bound up his wounds, pouring in oil and wine, and set him on his own beast and brought him to an inn, and took care of him. And on the morrow when he departed, he took out two pence, and gave them to the host, and said unto him. Take care of him; and whatsoever thou spendest more, when I come again, I will repay it."

The Good Samaritan, of course, pictures Christ. He finds the sinner half dead, used and abused by sin. He picks him up, nurses his wounds, and places him at the local *inn*, picturing perhaps, the local church, for care and safe keeping while He is gone away.

The Good Samaritan pays only two pence, or *two days* charges, indicating that the innkeeper may expect his return (when I come again) when the two days have expired.

Using Peter's time scale, prophetically, the Church might expect Christ to be gone for the space of, and to return at the end of *two days*, or two thousand years.

Listen to the language of Hosea 6:1-2, "Come, and let us return unto the LORD: for He hath torn, and He will heal us; He hath smitten and He will bind us up. After *two days* will He revive us: in the third day we shall live in His sight."

Here is the voice of the Jewish remnant in the last days. Notice that Israel is to spend *two days* "torn" and "smitten," and separated from God. Prophetically, Israel may expect that when the *two days* are finished, they will be revived, raised up, and shall live in God's sight.

The message seems to be the same for the Church and for Israel. The Church will have *two days*, or two thousand years in which to conduct her activities. During these two days Israel will remain torn and smitten as wanderers among the nations. When the *two days*, or two thousand years are finished, the Church will cross to be with Christ. Soon afterwards Israel will be regathered, restored and redeemed.

That she may expect her Lord's return when the two thousand years are expired would appear to be an exciting revelation for the Church, especially since we have already come to the close of the twentieth century.

It may be very possible that the two thousand years do represent the general time of Christ's coming for His Church. It may not be quite as likely, however, that they reveal the specific time for His return.

This is true primarily because verse 4 of Joshua Chapter 3 does not say that the "space" between the Ark and the people was to be exactly two thousand cubits. It says that the "space" was to be "ABOUT" two thousand cubits. This means it could have been somewhat more; it could have been somewhat less.

The language does not indicate that they actually stretched out a measuring tape and marked off exactly 2,000 cubits. The designation "ABOUT two thousand cubits" seems to allow for a good estimate of that distance. It may have been a little more. It may have been a little less. We do not know how much more or how much less.

Taken typologically and prophetically, the passage does seem to indicate that if the "space" in distance between the Ark and the people was ABOUT two thousand cubits, then the "space" in time between Christ's departure and the departure of the Church would be ABOUT two thousand years. That seems to be a good estimate. It could be a little more; it could be a little less. We do not know how much more or how much less.

It is no secret that some Bible students in the past thought in terms of two thousand years between Christ's first coming and His second coming. To count two thousand years from the birth of Christ would arrive at a date now past, that is, if the calendar which we presently use is anywhere near correct. According to Ussher's chronology Christ's birth was about 4 BC. Two thousand years from that date would have been 1996 AD.

If the "space" of two thousand cubits can be taken to represent a period of two thousand years, where should it be measured from.

In our text the two thousand cubits are not associated

with the High Priest's birth, they are associated with his crossing into the Jordan with the ark and the sacrificial blood. This would more correctly represent the time of Christ's ascension into Heaven.

Given that Christ's birth date was about 4 BC, and given that He lived about thirty three and one half years, the date of His departure or ascension into Heaven would have been about 30 AD. The "space" of two thousand years from that date would bring us to about 2030 AD.

Would 2030 AD, then, mark the date of Christ's return? Certainly, the period from 30 AD to 2030 AD does represent a "space" of two thousand years. Could this then be taken to be the date for Christ's coming? Could it be an approximation? Perhaps, but not an exact date.

Just as in Joshua 3:4 the "space" for Israel's crossing was not exactly two thousand cubits, but ABOUT two thousand cubits, so for the Church, the "space" for her crossing is probably not exactly two thousand years, but about two thousand years.

For Israel at the Jordan the crossing could have been a little more or a little less than two thousand cubits. We do not know how much more or how much less. And so for the Church, the time for Christ's return may not be exactly two thousand years. It may be a little more, or it may be a little less. We do not know how much more or how much less.

For the Church, the "space" might be a little longer than the two thousand years, a little beyond 2030 AD; or the "space" might be less than the two thousand years, which might place Christ's coming at any time between now and 2030 AD.

The scripture passages, Joshua 3:4, Luke 10:35 and Hosea 6:2 do seem to give an approximation of the time for Christ's return, ABOUT two thousand years, but the Church knows that she cannot set an exact date for Christ's return for He Himself said, "of that day and hour knoweth no man, no, not the angels of heaven, but my Father only." (Matthew 24:36)

One thing does seem to be certain, if we make it to the two thousand mark, wherever it is to be measured from, it cannot be much longer.

## "for tomorrow the LORD will do wonders among you"

Notice, first of all, the character of the crossing of the Jordan. The crossing would be a "wonder." The word used here is "pawlaw" from the Strong's word no. 6381. It means something that is very great, difficult, wonderful, marvelous, miraculous.

The verse says, "for tomorrow *the LORD* will do *wonders* among you." The crossing will be of such a miraculous nature that only Jehovah could accomplish it.

Their fathers, and many of them as children, had witnessed the *wonders* of Jehovah in Egypt, and how that finally, the Lord had redeemed them by the blood of the lamb out of the iron furnace and from the bondage of the hard taskmaster. Everyone of them had witnessed the wonders of Jehovah daily as their lives were sustained throughout the wilderness journey by the bread from heaven and the water from the rock. Every step of the way they had journeyed through the wonderful providential grace and the miraculous protecting power of The LORD God of Israel. And now they are assured that the crossing to Canaan would be nothing less than a marvelous **wonder**.

Very much like Israel, the Church has been redeemed by the Blood of the Lamb. She has been delivered from the bondage of sin and Satan, and from hell itself. She too has been sustained through her wilderness journey by the Bread of Heaven and the Water of Life. She too has daily experienced God's providential grace and protecting power. For the Church of the Heavenly Joshua, the Lord Jesus Christ, "the crossing" to the Father's House will be nothing less than a marvelous wonder.

Perhaps, even, the word *wonder* is given here in the plural, *"wonders,"* in anticipation of the two crossings: Israel's Old Testament crossing to Canaan, and prophetically, the Church's future crossing to Heaven.

Notice, also, the time given for crossing of the Jordan. The crossing was to be "tomorrow." Today was to be the day to hear the message and to prepare for the crossing. Tomorrow was to be the time to make the crossing. It is interesting to note that tomorrow comes when the "sun" appears. Likewise, for the Church, today, or "now, is the day of salvation." (2 Corinthians 6:2) Tomorrow is the time for the crossing. For the Church, tomorrow will come when the "son" appears.

For Israel at the Jordan *tomorrow* was going to be the *fifth* day since they had removed from Shittim and had come to lodge there. Verse one says, "they removed from Shittim, and came to Jordan, he and all the children of Israel, and lodged there before they passed over."

Even though their desire was to cross immediately, for three full days they did nothing but wait on God. Then after the three days, the officers spent the entire fourth day going through the host to command the people to watch for the Ark and to prepare for the crossing. On the fifth day they made the crossing.

What significance might this *fifth* day have for the Church as she waits to make the crossing? What New Testament truths might be hidden here?

One simple message of the *fifth* day is that the five days at the Jordan might represent for the Church the number five as the number of grace. Certainly, it is commonly accepted in dispensational teaching that the Church Period or The Church Age is The Grace Period or The Grace Age.

Since it is Israel in our text which pictures for us the Church, there may be even more significance in the five days, when we consider the special days which God gave to Israel. On the Jewish Calendar we see that God gave Israel seven special Days. These were her Feast days, her Holy Days. These seven Holy Days became known as The Seven Feasts of Israel.

The first three Days or Feasts were The Feast of the Passover, The Feast of Unleavened Bread and The Feast of The First Fruits. (Leviticus 23)

The Feast of Passover was the day when a lamb was slain, and speaks to us of Christ crucified. The Feast of Unleavened Bread reminds us of Christ own words, "this is my body," and it speaks to us of Christ buried. At The

Feast of First Fruits, the first plants which came up from the ground where they had been planted, were brought to the Lord's house, "on the morrow after the sabbath" (Leviticus 23:11), that is, on a Sunday morning, and they speak to us of Christ resurrected.

The first three Holy Days, or Feasts, speak to us of Christ's death, burial and resurrection. The Apostle Paul tells us that in reality this is the gospel, "that Christ died for our sins according to the scriptures; And that He was buried, and that He rose again the third day according to the scriptures." (1 Corinthians 15:3-4)

In Joshua 3:1-5 the officers had no message to give until after the three days. In the same way The Church had no message to preach until after Christ died, was buried and rose again.

Israel's fourth special Day or Feast was the Day of Pentecost. This was the very day on which the Church was empowered by the Holy Spirit to go out, and to preach the gospel. "But ye shall receive power after that the Holy Ghost is come upon you: and ye shall be witnesses unto me both in Jerusalem, and in all Judaea, and in Samaria, and unto the uttermost part of the earth." (Acts 1:8)

Once the three Days representing Christ's death, burial, and resurrection had passed, the officers spent the entire Fourth Day, carrying the message. In the same way the Church has spent the time from the Holy Spirit's coming at Pentecost until now carrying the gospel into all the world.

Notice that it was only when this Fourth Day of commanding the host had come to a close that the Fifth Day came. On that Fifth Day the sun appeared, bringing with it that glad *tomorrow* in which Israel would cross the Jordan to the Promised Land.

Of course, Israel's fifth special Day or Feast was known as The Feast of Trumpets. For the Church this message is very clear.

First there will be the three days which will represent how that Christ will be crucified, buried and resurrected. Then there will be a fourth day to represent how that the gospel will be preached in all the world. Then when the age of gospel preaching has come to a close, there will be a fifth day, a glad *Tomorrow*, when the "son" will appear, the Trumpet will sound, and the Church of Jesus Christ will make the crossing to the other side.

The only reason the Church has not already crossed is that she is still preaching the gospel, and she is still waiting for the Trumpet. One day soon when the world least expects it, there will be a ta-da-ta-da, and the LORD will do wonders among you. The sleeping saints will awaken and rise from their beds of clay. The living saints will be changed. Together they will be caught up into the clouds to meet the LORD in the air. The Church will cross the Jordan to be with Jesus.

## "And Joshua said to the people, Sanctify yourselves;"

Notice that when the time came to cross the Jordan, those who had put their full faith and trust in the Blood on the Mercy Seat of the Ark of the Covenant of the Lord would cross over, but they would not cross *unsanctified*.

The word "sanctify" means to set apart to God, to purify, to consecrate, to make holy. Sanctification is the work of God whereby He sets men apart unto Himself. He purifies them, consecrates them, makes them Holy unto the Lord.

The Bible teaches that sanctification is the work of God, the Holy Spirit, in the life of every child of God. The work of sanctification is an Initial work, a Progressive work and a Final work.

Initial Sanctification takes place at the time of the new birth. In Acts 26:18 Paul says, "that they may receive forgiveness of sins . . . among them which *are sanctified* by faith." Saving faith sanctifies men to God.

Progressive Sanctification is an ongoing process in the life of the believer. Romans 15:16 says, "*being sanctified* by the Holy Ghost." The work of the Holy Spirit in the life of the believer is to continually set him apart to God, to purify him, to consecrate him, to make him holy.

Final Sanctification or ultimate sanctification is the complete or total purification and consecration of the believer into the holy state. "That He might *sanctify* and cleanse it with the washing of water by the word, that He might present it to Himself a glorious church, not having spot, or wrinkle, or any such thing; but *that it should be holy and without blemish.*" (Ephesians 5:26-27)

In the work of Initial Sanctification the believer has been delivered from the penalty of sin. In the work of Progressive Sanctification the believer is being delivered from the power of sin. In the work of Final Sanctification the believer will be delivered from the very presence of sin. "Flesh and blood (that is, corrupt, unchanged, unsanctified flesh and blood) cannot inherit the kingdom of God." (I Corinthians 15:50) But "when He shall appear, we shall be like Him; for we shall see Him as He is." (I John 3:2)

The good news for the Church is that when crossing time shall come, she will not cross unsanctified. The gospel age shall come to a close, "the trumpet shall sound, and the dead shall be raised incorruptible, and we shall be changed." We shall be like Him. We shall wake in His likeness, and shall be satisfied. (Psalm 17:15) The Lord will do wonders among us. We will be like Jesus. We shall finally, and forever, be *sanctified*!

## "the people removed from their tents, to pass over Jordan" (vs. 14)

Like their father Abraham who left the fertile plains of Mesopotamia, and the comfortable accommodations of Ur of Chaldees, Israel in the wilderness dwelled, not in ceiled houses, but in tents.

Life for the desert nomads who dwelled only in tents was harsh and rugged at best. From well to well they journeyed looking for a city, or perhaps a land of promise, a place where they could fold their tents and settle down to the comforts of home. This was the sweet prospect which awaited the people of God just on the other side of Jordan.

Israel, once sanctified. removed from their tents to pass over Jordan. They were leaving behind four hundred harsh years in Egypt, and forty years in the wilderness. They were leaving behind the fear of hunger and thirst. They were leaving behind the blistering days and the freezing nights. They were leaving behind the howling winds and the drifting sands. They were leaving behind a barren land of death and dying where all the men of age who had come out of Egypt perished in the wilderness. And now they were entering in upon the promises of God. "The people removed from their tents to pass over Jordan."

For the Church, when crossing time shall come, she will leave this world of labor and toil, of trials and temptations, of sorrow and heartache, of fear and failure, of death and dying far behind. All her battles here will be fought. Her race on this side will be run. Her earthly labors will be ended. Her frail tent here will be folded. Her "earthly house of this tabernacle" will be dissolved, and she will enter into "a building of God, an house not made with hands, eternal in the heavens." (2 Corinthians 5:1) She will enter into rest in that continuing city (Hebrews 13:14), that New Jerusalem which the Lord has gone to prepare. She will remove from her tent to pass over Jordan.

## "Jordan overfloweth all his banks all the time of harvest." (vs.15)

For Israel, crossing time came. It was a happy time. It was the Hebrew month of Nisan. It was Passover time, a time of celebrating their redemption out of the bondage of Egypt by the blood of the lamb.

It was springtime. It was the time of year when all creation was undergoing a resurrection. Winter was past. The trees were "shooting forth," "the fig tree and all the trees" (Luke 21:29-31)

It was the time of the harvest of the winter barley crop. It was the very same time of the year when a yet future Hebrew Boaz would take a Moabitish damsel to be his bride.

For the Church crossing time will come. It will be a happy time, a time for celebrating her redemption out of the bondage of sin and condemnation by the blood of the Lamb of God which taketh away the sin of the world.

For the Church crossing time will be a time of resurrection. Triumphantly, the dead in Christ will awaken from their beds of clay together with "we which are alive and remain" to be changed into Christ's own image and caught up to meet him in the air

For the Church crossing time will be a time when the trees are shooting forth, that is when nations are rising, especially "the fig tree." In scripture "the fig tree" always pictures National Israel, that is, Israel, as a nation.

Today, Israel is restored as a nation after nearly 1900 years of dispersion. Other trees have shot forth. In other words, Bible prophecies have been fulfilled. The nations spoken of in the prophetic Word have risen to power and are in place. The stage is set for the end time.

For the Church crossing time will come at harvest time. Israel crossed the Jordan in harvest time. The barley harvest everywhere in scripture speaks of the ingathering of the Jewish remnant, the harvest of Israel. It spoke importantly of the harvest of the Old Testament saints just before Christ Our Passover was offered for us at the beginning of the Church period. The Church, in Joshua 3, pictured by Israel at the Jordan, crosses, or is harvested out, so that God's program for Israel may resume, so that the harvest of the remnant of Israel may be gathered in.

For the Church crossing time will be a time of marriage. It was during the barley harvest, that is, at the very same time of year which Israel crossed the Jordan that the man from Bethlehem, the owner of the fields, the heir of Judah, the Jewish Boaz appeared to redeem and consummate his marriage to the to the Moabitess, Ruth.

And it will be at crossing time that the Heavenly Boaz will make his appearance to redeem the believers of this present age, as Romans 8: 23 says, ". . . even we ourselves groan within ourselves, waiting for. . . the redemption of our body." take the predominately Gentile Church to be His Bride.

For Israel at the Jordan it was an exciting time, knowing that just any moment now they would be in the Land of Promise. They were close enough to feel the breezes from the other side. They were close enough to hear the bees buzzing, and to smell the honey from Canaan's good land.

How exciting for the Church to know that she stands on the brink of the crossing to the Land of her Dreams!

For Israel at the Jordan it was an exciting time, but it was also a fearful time, because the Jordan was *"overflowing all his banks."*

One of the dangers of the swelling Jordan was that it drove the wild animals back from the river, and they often came out of hiding and into the villages to make a prey of the people.

Jeremiah 50:44 says, "Behold, he shall come up like a lion from the swelling of Jordan unto the habitation of the strong." The prophecy here concerns the King of Babylon, and is very like the prophecies of the "beasts" to rise at the end time which are foretold in Revelation 13-19.

The beast and the false prophet will be ready to come out of hiding, "like a lion at the swelling of Jordan" when the time comes for the Church to make her crossing.

Many other fearful conditions already exist. The apostle Paul warned of them in II Timothy 3:1-7, "This know also, that in the last days perilous times shall come. For men shall be lovers of their own selves, covetous, boasters, proud, blasphemers, disobedient to parents, unthankful, unholy, Without natural affection, truce-breakers, false accusers, incontinent, fierce, despisers of those that are good, Traitors, heady, high-minded, lovers of pleasures more than lovers of God; Having a form of godliness, but denying the power thereof: from such turn away. For of this sort are they which creep into houses, and lead captive silly women laden with sins, led away with divers lusts, Ever learning, and never able to come to the knowledge of the truth."

This warning certainly describes the time in which we live. It is an exciting time, but it is a fearful time. The Jordan is overflowing all of her banks. The cup of man's sin is full and overflowing.

But Christ, our Great High Priest, has gone down to the Jordan with the Blood of The Eternal Covenant, and has made a way for His people to cross over.

Throughout her history, The Church has had to face fearful times. In spite of it all, through the centuries, The True Church has marched on. The gates of Hell have not prevailed against The Church of the Living God.

Now two thousand years are well nigh past. The waters stand up heaps upon heaps. Crossing time has come. It is the time for the harvest. It is the day of wild beasts. It is time for Jacob's trouble. It is resurrection time. The wedding feast is prepared. The Church stands ready to cross The Jordan!

## "the priests . . . shall stand still in Jordan"

The command for the priests in verse 8 was: "When ye are come to the brink of the water of Jordan, ye shall stand still in Jordan." The priests with Ark of the Covenant were not to *cross over* Jordan, but to pass "*into* Jordan."

The priests with the High Priest leading the procession took up the Ark, went down to the Jordan, and stepped into the waters. The waters of the Jordan were parted. The priests passed into the Jordan.

"And the priests that bare the Ark of the covenant of the Lord stood firm on dry ground in the midst of Jordan, and all the Israelites passed over on dry ground, until all the people were passed clean over Jordan."

At the moment the priests stepped into the Jordan, the people stood about two thousand cubits away from their own crossing. Then each step they took, brought them one step nearer the crossing.

They counted one cubit up to ten cubits, ten cubits up to a hundred cubits, a hundred cubits up through a thousand cubits, a thousand cubits up to two thousand cubits. Each step, each cubit brought the Israelites one step closer to that final step into the Jordan, and then, home at last.

In the same way, The Church has counted the years, the decades, the centuries and the millenia, and has come now very nearly to her final step into the great divide, and then, home to be with Jesus.

Standing there with eyes full of wonder, and hearts filled with anticipation, on the Jordan's bank, when the time had finally come for the crossing, all the people crossed together at the same time.

When the time finally comes for the Church to make the crossing, all the believers from the beginning until the ending of this age will cross together at the same time.

Notice that the priests did not cross to Canaan before the people, but were waiting at the river for their arrival. Likewise, the Lord Jesus Christ, our Great High Priest will be waiting at the river to welcome each believer as he crosses into the Heavenly Canaan. The song writer said it right, "In the darkness I see, He'll be waiting for me. I won't have to cross Jordan alone."

The High Priest of Israel lived a very secret, sheltered life, shut up unto God, separated from the people, serving in and around the Tabernacle. He was never seen by the average person.

In the same way Hebrews 7:26 says that "such an High Priest became us, who is holy, harmless, undefiled separate from sinners and made higher than the heavens." I Peter 1:8 says, "Whom having not seen, ye love."

Few in Israel had ever seen their High Priest although their fortunes and futures depended upon the offerings and the intercessions which He made for them hidden from their view inside that secret holy place at the tabernacle in the wilderness.

But when the time finally came for Israel to make the crossing over the Jordan, their High Priest was standing in the Jordan, waiting to welcome them home. Every Israelite was allowed the blessed privilege of seeing him face to face.

For the Church, the vast majority have never seen Christ, although our fortunes and futures depend upon His offering and His intercession for us hidden away in Heaven in that "true tabernacle, which the Lord pitched and not man." (Hebrews 8:2)

Only the few who were here during His earthly life and ministry were privileged to see the Lord Jesus. But when the time comes for the Church to make the crossing, every born again, blood washed, child of "God, shall see Him face to face. I Corinthians 13:12, "For now we see through a glass darkly; but then face to face."

## "Come ye up out of Jordan."

When the time finally came for Israel to cross the Jordan, Chapter 4:15-16, says, "And the LORD spake unto Joshua, saying, Command the priests that bear the ark of the testimony, that they *come up out of* Jordan. Verse 17 says, "Joshua therefore commanded the priests, saying, ***Come ye up out of*** Jordan." Verse 18 says, "And it came to pass, when the priests that bare the ark of the covenant of the LORD were *come up out of* the midst of Jordan. . ." And verse 19 says, "And the people *came up out of* Jordan."

Two directional terms are used to describe The Crossing of the Jordan: *up* and *out of*.

They are the very same terms used in the New Testament for Jesus' return to the Father's house at the close of His ministry here.

Notice the use of the term *up*. Luke 9:51, "And it came to pass, when the time was come that he should be received *up*, he steadfastly set his face to go to Jerusalem. Mark 16:19, "So then after the Lord had spoken unto them, he was received *up* into heaven, and sat on the right hand of God."

Notice the use of the term *out of*. John 13:1, Now before the feast of the passover, when Jesus knew that His hour was come that He should depart *out of* this world unto the Father, having loved His own which were in the world, He loved them unto the end.

When crossing time came for Israel, the LORD was not on the wilderness side of the river saying, go up out of Jordan and into Canaan; but from the text, Jehovah Himself was already on the Canaan side saying to the people *come ye up out of* Jordan to Canaan. When crossing time comes for the Church, believers will *come up out of* this world and return with Jesus to the Father's house.

I Thessalonians 4:13-18, bears this out: "But I would not have you to be ignorant, brethren, concerning them which are asleep, that ye sorrow not, even as others which have no hope. For if we believe that Jesus died and rose again, even so them also which sleep in Jesus will God bring with him. For this we say unto you by the word of the Lord, that we which are alive and remain unto the coming of the Lord shall not prevent them which are asleep. For the Lord Himself shall descend from heaven with a shout, with the voice of the archangel, and with the trump of God: and the dead in Christ shall rise first: Then we which are alive and remain shall be *caught up* together with them in the clouds, to meet the Lord in the air: and so shall we ever be with the Lord. Wherefore comfort one another with these words."

## "And the people came up out of Jordan."

Do not miss this one all important truth about the crossing of the Jordan. It happened!

In Chapter 4:19 of Joshua, that which for centuries had been just a promise, first given to Abraham in Genesis 15:13-14, and then to Moses in Exodus 3:6-8 had now become a reality. What had been only a hope had now come to pass. The people came up out of Jordan!

God's promises may not always be immediately

fulfilled. They are not always meant to soon come to pass. But "The Lord is not slack concerning His promise, as some men count slackness; but is longsuffering to usward, not willing that any should perish, but that all should come to repentance." (2 Peter 3:9)

The people of Israel wanted to cross the Jor-dan the first day they came to it. They did not want to remain in the wilderness one day longer than necessary. But so many were not even aware that they had reached the Jordan, and had not heard the message of the Ark of the Covenant of the LORD. They needed to hear the message of the atoning blood, of the interceding Highpriest, and to make the preparation for the crossing.

How wonderful it would be if Christ were to come today and to take The Church home to Glory, but so many have never heard the message and are not prepared to make the crossing.

Christ will come in due time, but remember the words of the Apostle Peter. "Wherefore beloved, seeing that ye look for such things, be diligent that ye may be found of Him in peace, without spot, and blameless. And account that the longsuffering of our Lord is salvation." (2 Peter 3:14-15)

The one and only one reason that Christ has not already come is given in James 5:7, "Behold the husbandman waiteth for the precious fruit of the earth, and hath long patience for it." The Lord the great husbandman is waiting for the harvest to be completed. And we are encouraged in James 5:8, "Be ye also patient stablish your hearts for the coming of the Lord draweth nigh."

Rest assured our Lord does not and will not delay His coming. "For yet a little while, and He that shall come will come, and will not tarry." (Hebrews 10:37) It will happen!!

## "all the people passed. . . clean over Jordan."

In Joshua 3:17 "clean" means "completely." All the people passed completely over Jordan. Not one Israelite was left behind. No one was lost along the way. Thank God that in Christ His people are secure. In John 17:12, Jesus says, "those that thou gavest me I have kept, and none of them is lost."

The Apostle Paul under the inspiration of the Holy Spirit penned these words, "Nevertheless the foundation of God standeth sure, having this seal, The Lord knoweth them that are His." (2 Timothy 2:19) The Good Shepherd knows His sheep, and "He calleth His own sheep by name, and leadeth them out." (John 10:3) He is the Shepherd who never lost a sheep. Here and now He is leading them out to green pastures, but one day He will lead them *out of* this world, and *up* to the Heavenly fold.

What a blessing to know that in Heaven all the Church, every saved person, every child of God, every battle weary saint will be present and accounted for.

**"And Joshua rose early in the morning; and they removed from Shittim, and came to Jordan, he and all the children of Israel, and lodged there before they passed over."**

The people came to Jordan. There for the last time they set up camp. There they heard once more the message of the Ark of God with its Blood Splattered Mercy Seat. There they looked to the Great High Priest who made sacrifice for them, and interceded for them before the vail. There He led them on to The Crossing Of The Jordan!

The Church has now come very nearly to the end of the age. She has set up camp as it were for what could very well be the last time. She is looking to, and faithfully proclaiming the message of The Lord Jesus Christ who for us all offered His "one sacrifice for sin forever." (Hebrews 10:12) What a blessed day it will be when The Church's Great High priest will lead her safely on to The Crossing Of The Jordan.

# TO BE READY FOR THE CROSSING
# YOU MUST REALIZE THAT:

**GOD HAS PROVIDED FOR SALVATION**
"For God so loved the world, that He gave His only begotten son, that whosoever believeth in Him should not perish, but have everlasting life." John 3:16 "For by grace are ye saved, through faith, and that not of yourselves, it is the gift of God." Ephesians 2:8

**ALL MEN NEED TO BE SAVED**
"For all have sinned, and come short of the glory of God." Romans 3:23 "Except a man be born again, he cannot see the Kingdom of God." John 3:3

**MEN CANNOT SAVE THEMSELVES**
"For whosoever shall keep the whole law, and yet offend in one point, he is guilty of all." James 2:10 "By the deeds of the law there shall no flesh be justified in His sight: for by the law is the knowledge of sin." Romans 3:20 "Not of works lest any man should boast." Ephesians 2:9

**MEN MUST REPENT**
"And that repentance and remission of sins should be preached in His name among all nations, beginning at Jerusalem." Luke 24:47 ". . . But now commandeth all men every where to repent: " Acts 17:30 "I tell you, Nay: but, except ye repent, ye shall all likewise perish." Luke 13:3,5

**MEN MUST TRUST CHRIST**
"Jesus answered and said unto them, This is the work of God, that ye believe In Him whom He hath sent." John 6:29 "Verily, verily, I say unto you, He that heareth my word, and believeth on Him that sent me, hath everlasting life,
and shall not come into condemnation, but is passed from death unto life." John 5:24

**TRUE FAITH BRINGS TRUE CONVERSION**
"Therefore if any man be in Christ, he is a new creature: old things are passed away, behold all things are become new." 2 Corinthians 5:17 "For the grace of God that bringeth salvation hath appeared to all men, teaching us that, denying ungodliness and worldly lusts, we should live soberly, righteously, and godly, in this present world, looking for that blessed hope, and the glo-rious appearing of the great God and our Saviour Jesus Christ." Titus 2:11-13

## Other Books By This Author

**Summer Is Almost Here**
**The Story Of The Stones**
**God's Dynamite!**

The Voice of Truth Ministries
Longpoint Baptist Church
PO Box 310
Anawalt, West Virginia 24808

(304) 383-2246